PASSION

BELIEF

ACHIEVEMENT

YOUR MINDSET IS YOUR GREATEST WEAPON

Volume 1

COACH P.JIM PUSATERI

Visit the Author online at:
<u>www.Inspiringthem.com</u>

PAPERBACK ISBN: 979-8-9942-5572-8

Contents

Episode 1 1

   PASSION: THE FIRE THAT STARTS YOUR JOURNEY 1

Episode 2 11

   BELIEF: THE ENGINE OF ACHIEVEMENT 11

Episode 3 21

   OVERCOMING MENTAL BLOCKS.. 21

Episode 4 30

   ACHIEVEMENT: TURNING YOUR EFFORT INTO RESULTS................. 30

Episode 5 38

   TURNING SMALL WINS INTO BIG WINS 38

Episode 6 46

   PURSUING YOUR PURPOSE WITH INTENTIONALITY 46

   TODAY'S PURPOSE CHALLENGE.. 54

Episode 7 55

   IDENTIFYING WHAT'S HOLDING YOU BACK 55

Episode 8 64

   HOW TO BUILD UNBREAKABLE CONSISTENCY............................... 64

Episode 9 73

   DISCIPLINE OVER MOTIVATION 73

Episode 10 80

   LEARNING TO TRUST YOURSELF AGAIN 80

   HOW OUR COURSES BUILD SELF-TRUST 87

Episode 11 89

   CONTROLLING THE CONTROLLABLES.. 89

Episode 12 99

   BUILDING RESILIENCE: BOUNCING BACK STRONGER 99

Episode 1

PASSION: THE FIRE THAT STARTS YOUR JOURNEY

Welcome to the first chapter of Mental Performance Series Book.

I'm Coach P — Jim Pusateri — and today we are kicking off this entire series with one of the most important pillars of success:

Passion.

Passion is your fire.

It's your spark.

It's the energy inside of you that says:

> "This matters."

> "This is who I am."

> "This is what I'm meant to do."

But passion isn't just excitement.

It's not hype.

It's not a burst of emotion.

True passion is your internal compass — the thing that points you toward your purpose.

Today, we're going deeper than the surface.

We're going to talk about:

How to identify your passion

How passion connects to mental toughness

Why most people lose passion

How to reignite it

And how passion ties into the journey of achievement you're about to take with us

This Chapter sets the foundation for everything that follows.

Let's get started.

WHAT PASSION REALLY IS

A lot of people misunderstand passion.

Passion isn't hype.

Passion isn't intensity.

Passion isn't motivation.

Passion is a pull — not a push.

It pulls you forward, even when you're tired.

It pulls you out of bed, even when life gets heavy.

It pulls you toward the work that matters, even on your worst days.

In Mental Toughness by Coach P Podcast, I talk about how true passion gives your life energy, purpose, and direction.

Without it, people drift.

They settle.

They live below their potential.

But with passion?

You gain:

- Drive
- Courage
- Consistency
- Resilience
- Commitment
- Vision
- Passion lights the path.
- Mental toughness keeps you on it.

THE THREE COMPONENTS OF PASSION

Passion is made of three parts:

1. What Comes Naturally to You

What do you love doing?

What energizes you?

What feels effortless?

2. What You Care Deeply About

What matters to you?

What causes move your heart?

What problems do you feel called to solve?

3. What You're Willing to Struggle For

This is the big one — the separator.

Anybody can love something when it's easy.

Passion becomes real ONLY when it's tested through:

- Obstacle
- Frustration
- Pain
- Pressure
- Delay
- Failure
- Passion is proven through adversity.

WHY PEOPLE LOSE PASSION

People lose passion for several reasons:

1. Life Distracts Them

Bills. Responsibility. Stress. Survival mode.

Life gets busy — passion gets buried.

2. They Stop Growing

When you stop growing, passion suffocates.

Growth feeds passion.

Stagnation kills it.

3. They Follow Expectations Instead of Calling

Many people live someone else's plan instead of their own.

They become:

Who their parents wanted

Who society wanted

Who their job wanted

Who their past shaped them to be

But passion requires alignment with who you truly are.

4. They Forget Their "Why"

When your "why" fades, passion fades with it.

5. Their Self-Belief Drops

If you don't believe you can achieve your passion,

you'll stop pursuing it.

This is why our Mindset / Mental Performance Course is such a game-changer — it rebuilds the belief system that passion depends on.

REDISCOVERING YOUR PASSION

Here are the steps to reignite your passion:

STEP 1 — Go Back to What Lit You Up as a Kid

Before the world told you who to be...

Before responsibilities piled up...

What did you naturally gravitate toward?

This is clue #1.

STEP 2 — Look at Where You Lose Track of Time

When you are fully immersed —

that's passion revealing itself.

STEP 3 — Listen to What Makes You Come Alive

Something inside you says:

"This is me."

"This feels right."

"This matters."

Follow that.

STEP 4 — Pay Attention to What You're Drawn to Learn

If you love learning about something,

that's passion calling.

STEP 5 — Identify the Work Worth Struggling For

Remember — passion is what you're willing to fight for.

If you're not willing to struggle for it, it's not passion — it's a hobby.

THE ROLE OF PASSION IN ACHIEVEMENT

Achievement is not a straight line.

It's a climb — filled with:

- Setbacks
- Uncertainty
- Fatigue
- Frustration
- Delays
- Obstacles
- Pressure

Passion is the fuel that keeps you climbing.

In the Mental Performance Series we're creating — starting with Booklet 1: Passion, Belief & Achievement — passion is the very first building block because:

You cannot pursue greatness without caring deeply about the path.

Achievement requires effort.

Effort requires energy.

Energy comes from passion.

***

HOW OUR ONLINE COURSES HELP YOU FIND AND BUILD PASSION

We didn't create those courses by accident — each one plays a key role:

THE PASSION COURSE — Finding Your Dream Job

Helps you uncover your gifts, your calling, and the work that aligns with your identity.

THE GOAL SETTING COURSE

Once passion gives you direction, this course gives you a roadmap.

THE MINDSET / MENTAL PERFORMANCE COURSE

You can know your passion and still sabotage yourself.

This course rewires confidence, self-talk, and daily habits.

Together, these courses create a powerful system that fuels your passion AND supports the discipline needed to pursue it.

THE PASSION CHECKLIST

Here is your assignment for today — a quick test to determine if something is truly your passion:

Ask yourself:

✓ Does it energize me?

✓ Does it feel natural to me?

✓ Does it excite me to learn about it?

✓ Does it matter deeply to me?

✓ Would I do it even if it got difficult?

✓ Does it align with the person I want to become?

If the answer is YES to at least four of these —

you've found your passion.

TURNING PASSION INTO PURPOSE

Passion is the fire.

Purpose is the direction.

Mental toughness is the vehicle.

When passion meets purpose — you become unstoppable.

This is the heart of your entire Mental Performance journey.

This is the heart of our podcast.

This is the heart of your upcoming 10-book series.

This is the heart of your life's mission.

Your passion is the spark that begins your climb.

Don't ignore it.

Don't silence it.

Don't bury it.

Follow it.

Fuel it.

Grow it.

Protect it.

Passion will lead you to the life you're meant to live — and mental toughness will help you reach it.

Let's move forward.

Let's chase purpose.

Let's build greatness.

And as always...

Let's keep climbing.

✳✳✳

Episode 2

BELIEF: THE ENGINE OF ACHIEVEMENT

Welcome back to the Mental Toughness Podcast.

Let's talk about something that determines EVERY outcome in your life:

Belief.

Belief is the engine behind everything you do.

You cannot outperform it.

You cannot rise above it.

You cannot achieve long-term success without it.

Belief determines your:

✓ Confidence

✓ Identity

✓ Performance

✓ Resilience

✓ Direction

✓ Decisions

✓ Habits

✓ Future

If passion lights the fire,

belief is what keeps the fire burning.

Let's explore:

What belief really is

Why most people struggle with it

How belief gets damaged

How to rebuild it

And how belief shapes your future identity

Let's dive in.

WHAT BELIEF REALLY IS

Belief is not positive thinking.

Belief is not hype.

Belief is not pretending everything is perfect.

Belief is trust in your ability to grow.

Belief says:

"I can figure this out."

"I can get better."

"I can become stronger."

"I can climb through pressure."

"I can achieve the goals I set."

Belief is not about knowing the whole path.

It's about trusting yourself to take the next step.

In Mental Toughness by Coach P Podcast, I talk about how belief is built through evidence — through the actions you take, the promises you keep, and the identity you reinforce.

You are always building belief.

The question is:

Are you building belief in your strength or belief in your limitations?

HOW BELIEF GETS SHAKEN

People don't lose belief overnight.

It gets chipped away slowly.

Belief weakens when you:

Quit on yourself

Break your own promises

Repeat the same habits you want to change

Let fear make decisions

Fail and never try again

Surround yourself with negative people

Compare yourself endlessly

Stay in environments that don't support growth

Forget your purpose

Every time you say "I can't,"

your belief shrinks.

Every time you take action,

your belief grows.

THE BELIEF TRIANGLE

Belief is made of three components:

1. Identity — Who You Think You Are

If you see yourself as:

Undisciplined

Inconsistent

Weak

Unorganized

Not enough

...your behavior will always match that identity.

Identity is the software of your mind.

You must upgrade it if you want new results.

2. Evidence — What You Repeatedly Do

Your brain believes what you do consistently.

If you:

Show up

Work hard

Stay disciplined

Keep promises

Make progress

...your mind forms evidence that you CAN.

But if you avoid hard things, your brain forms evidence that you WON'T.

3. Environment — Who and What Influences You

Your environment can strengthen or destroy your belief.

If you surround yourself with:

Complainers

Quitters

Negative thinkers

Unambitious people

...your belief will collapse.

If you surround yourself with:

Builders

Leaders

Positive energy

Growth mindset individuals

...your belief will expand.

This is why your Mental Performance journey matters so much — the right environment builds belief.

BELIEF AND YOUR FUTURE SELF

The future you want requires a new belief system.

Think about the person you want to become in:

1 year

5 years

10 years

Does that version of you think small?

Quit early?

Fear failure?

Avoid discomfort?

Or does that version of you:

Show up

Push through

Take risks

Lead with confidence

Take responsibility

Follow through

Trust the process

Belief is becoming.

Belief is the bridge between who you are now and who you are becoming.

✳✳✳

HOW TO STRENGTHEN YOUR BELIEF SYSTEM

Here are the exact steps I teach in our Mindset & Mental Performance Course:

STEP 1 — Change Your Self-Talk

Your self-talk is your story.

Rewrite the script:

"I can improve."

"I can figure this out."

"I can learn this."

"I am capable."

"I am stronger than this challenge."

Your mind listens to your voice more than anyone else's.

STEP 2 — Create Small Daily Wins

Small wins build belief.

Belief builds confidence.

Confidence builds performance.

This is why the Mental Performance Series emphasizes micro-actions — because small wins compound into unstoppable belief.

STEP 3 — Keep One Promise to Yourself Daily

Just one.

The fastest way to destroy belief is to break promises.

The fastest way to rebuild belief is to keep them.

STEP 4 — Use Failure as Evidence, Not Judgment

Failure is information.

Failure is direction.

Failure is HOW belief grows.

You don't build belief by avoiding difficulty.

You build belief by facing difficulty and surviving it.

STEP 5 — Surround Yourself with Growth

Faith is contagious.

Belief is contagious.

Energy is contagious.

If you want stronger belief, surround yourself with stronger believers — our podcast, your courses, your upcoming mental performance books — these are all environments designed to grow belief.

HOW OUR COURSES BUILD BELIEF

All three courses support your belief in different ways:

1. Passion: Finding Your Dream Job

Helps you believe in your future — your purpose and calling.

2. Goal Setting

Gives you structure and clarity so belief has a path to follow.

3. Mindset & Mental Performance

Builds the internal confidence and identity needed to stay consistent.

These courses don't just give you information.

They give you transformation by strengthening your belief system daily.

***

MENTAL PERFORMANCE SERIES BOOK

Every Chapter in the book reinforces belief:

 1: Passion, Belief & Achievement

 2: Overcoming Mental Blocks

 3: Building Consistency

 4: Goal Setting

 5: Leadership & Influence

And Chapters 6–10 on focus, discipline, courage, identity, and resilience

You are building belief piece by piece, episode by episode, book by Book

This is a system — and systems create lasting results.

Belief is the engine behind your effort.

Belief is the foundation of your confidence.

Belief is the start of your greatness.

If you can strengthen your belief,

you can strengthen your entire life.

So today:

Believe in your ability to grow.

Believe in your ability to change.

Believe in your ability to achieve.

Believe in the future you're building.

Now let's take the next step forward.

Let's build belief that can handle pressure.

And as always…

Let's keep climbing.

Episode 3

OVERCOMING MENTAL BLOCKS

I n this chapter we're talking about something every human being
faces, no matter their age, career, or background:

Mental Blocks.

Those invisible walls that show up when you're just about to grow.

Just about to take a step forward.

Just about to make progress.

And then suddenly — boom.

Your mind stops you.

Here's the truth:

Mental blocks aren't signs that you're weak.

They're signs that you're on the edge of growth.

In my book Mental Toughness by Coach P, and throughout the Mental
Performance online courses, I talk a lot about the internal obstacles
that get in the way of your progress. And this chapter will take those
teachings even deeper.

Today we're going to break down:

What mental blocks are

Why they appear

How to break through them

And how to prevent them from returning

PLUS — I'll show you how our upcoming Mental Performance Series of books is designed to help you unlock these breakthroughs with powerful, practical tools.

Let's get into it.

WHAT ARE MENTAL BLOCKS?

Mental blocks are INTERNAL barriers.

✓ Not physical.

✓ Not external.

✓ Internal.

They are the thoughts, fears, emotions, memories, or beliefs that interrupt your ability to move forward.

They often show up as:

- Fear
- Doubt
- Perfectionism
- Overthinking
- Low confidence
- Pressure
- Old failures replaying in your mind
- Uncertainty about the next step

You know that feeling:

You WANT to take action...

You KNOW what to do...

But something inside freezes you.

Mental blocks don't appear when life is easy.

They appear when you're stepping out of comfort — when you're stepping into growth.

That is why overcoming them is such a core part of mental toughness.

THE THREE TYPES OF MENTAL BLOCKS

There are three major categories:

1. Performance Blocks

These show up when pressure rises.

Maybe you're:

Trying to make a change

Stepping into a new role

Trying something new

Attempting a difficult task

Worried about failing in front of others

Your brain senses "threat" and tries to protect you — even though the threat is not real.

2. Emotional Blocks

Rooted in:

Past pain

Failed relationships

Embarrassment

Criticism

Being judged

Disappointments

Your emotions act like anchors.

3. Identity Blocks

This is the big one.

Identity blocks come from the story you tell yourself:

"I'm not good enough."

"I don't finish things."

"I'm not disciplined."

"I always mess things up."

"I'm not confident."

Identity is powerful — and the wrong identity can crush progress.

This is EXACTLY why this first book of the Mental Performance Series — Passion, Belief & Achievement — focuses heavily on identity transformation.

WHY MENTAL BLOCKS SHOW UP

Here are the three biggest reasons mental blocks appear:

1. You're stepping out of your comfort zone.

Growth activates resistance.

Your brain tries to pull you back to "safety."

Safety = familiarity, not progress.

2. You're overthinking instead of executing.

Overthinking is the enemy of action.

When there is too much thinking, there is too little movement.

3. You don't have a clear plan.

Lack of clarity breeds hesitation.

And this is why our Goal Setting Course is so powerful — it gives you structure, clarity, direction, and a daily action plan.

Clarity kills mental blocks.

Confusion feeds them.

THE MENTAL BLOCK BREAKTHROUGH FORMULA

This is the exact process we use with athletes, entrepreneurs, and leaders:

STEP 1 — Name the Block

You can't defeat what you won't acknowledge.

Say it out loud:

"I'm afraid of failing."

"I'm worried about judgment."

"I don't believe in myself yet."

"I'm unsure about the next step."

Naming the block takes away its power.

STEP 2 — Break It Down

Ask yourself:

"What is ONE small action I can take despite this block?"

Don't solve the whole problem.

Just break a piece off.

STEP 3 — Take Action Immediately

Not tomorrow.

Not next week.

Not after you feel ready.

NOW.

Action kills fear.

Action eliminates hesitation.

Action builds confidence.

And action is the core theme in all three of our online courses — because nothing changes without movement.

THE COACH P 4-MINUTE RESET

This is a simple daily practice designed to break through mental blocks in real time.

Minute 1 — Breathe

Slow, deep breathing calms the nervous system and clears mental fog.

Minute 2 — Identify the Block

Say:

"What exactly is stopping me right now?"

Minute 3 — Pick One Small Action

One thing.

Simple.

Achievable.

Minute 4 — Do It

Do something — ANYTHING — that moves you forward.

Motion defeats emotion.

***

THE TRUTH ABOUT MENTAL BLOCKS

Here's what most people don't realize:

Mental blocks are NOT real obstacles.

They are mental interpretations.

The block is not the event — it's your perception of the event.

In Mental Toughness by Coach P Podcast, we talk about how the mind creates protective stories disguised as obstacles:

"This might go wrong..."

"What will they think..."

"I'm not ready..."

"I'm not good enough..."

None of these are real.

They're mental filters — and filters can be changed.

You're not fighting a wall.

You're fighting a thought.

And thoughts can be replaced.

THE NIKE RULE: JUST START

You don't need courage.

You don't need confidence.

You don't need clarity.

You need movement.

That's why high performers don't wait for the "right moment."

They create momentum through action.

Take the step.

Do the thing.

Move forward under pressure.

Action dissolves the block.

Mental blocks don't define you.

They don't control you.

They don't own you.

You have the power to:

Name them

Break them down

Take action

Rewrite the story

Build confidence

Move forward under pressure

Your next level is waiting on the other side of the mental block that's in front of you right now.

Take the step.

Start with something small.

Build momentum.

Let's move forward.

Let's get better.

And as always...

Let's keep climbing.

Episode 4

ACHIEVEMENT: TURNING YOUR EFFORT INTO RESULTS

In this chapter we're breaking down a topic that everyone wants, but few understand how to actually achieve:

Achievement.

Achievement is not luck.

Achievement is not talent.

Achievement is not a gift someone hands you.

Achievement is a skill set.

Achievement is a mindset.

Achievement is a system.

And once you understand how achievement actually works, you can repeat it again and again — in your goals, your career, your relationships, your health, your leadership, and your life.

In Chapters 1, 2, and 3, we covered:

✓ Passion — your fire

✓ Belief — your engine

✓ Overcoming Mental Blocks — your breakthrough

In this chapter we connect the dots and show you how to convert your passion, belief, and action into real results.

This is a big one - Let's dive in.

WHAT ACHIEVEMENT ACTUALLY IS

Achievement is not success.

Success is an outcome.

Achievement is the process that gets you there.

Achievement is:

Showing up

Doing the work

Navigating obstacles

Staying consistent

Adjusting when needed

Moving forward under pressure

Achievement is the COMPILATION of daily decisions that lead to long-term results.

In Mental Toughness by Coach P Podcast, I talk about the internal game of achievement — how your mind determines your effort, and your effort determines your outcome.

Success is a product of who you become in the process.

***

THE ACHIEVEMENT PYRAMID

To achieve anything, you need three components:

1. Vision

You must know what you want.

Vision creates direction.

Direction creates focus.

Focus creates action.

This is why the Mental Performance Series Books will focus on Vision, Purpose, and Goal Setting.

Without clarity, achievement is impossible.

2. Process

Vision gives you the target —

process gives you the roadmap.

Your process includes:

Habits

Routines

Systems

Daily disciplines

Accountability

Standards

This is what turns your intentions into results.

3. Persistence

Nothing important is achieved quickly.

Achievement requires staying in the game when:

It's hard

You're tired

You're unsure

Progress slows

Pressure rises

Persistence is the separator.

The people who win are not always the most talented —

they are the most persistent.

WHY MOST PEOPLE DON'T ACHIEVE THEIR GOALS

There are four big reasons:

1. They set goals based on emotion, not structure.

Goals without a system are just wishes.

2. They expect fast results.

Real achievement takes time, consistency, and patience.

3. They stop when discomfort hits.

Achievement requires pushing through resistance.

4. They don't build an identity around the achievement.

Identity drives performance.

If you don't see yourself as someone who achieves — you won't.

This is why our Mindset & Mental Performance Course is so important — it rewires identity from the inside out.

THE ACHIEVEMENT LOOP

Here is the exact cycle high achievers follow:

STEP 1 — Set the Target

Clear. Specific. Measurable.

STEP 2 — Build the Process

Your habits and routines.

STEP 3 — Take Massive Daily Action

Small, consistent steps beat big, inconsistent effort.

STEP 4 — Review & Adapt

Check progress. Adjust strategies. Remove what isn't working.

STEP 5 — Reinforce the Identity

Tell yourself:

"I'm someone who follows through."

"I'm someone who finishes what I start."

"I'm someone who gets results."

Identity is the fuel of achievement.

***

THE HIDDEN TRUTH OF ACHIEVEMENT: DELAYED REWARD

Here's what most people don't realize:

Achievement is delayed.

You work today.

You grind today.

You build today.

But the results don't show up until later.

This is why belief matters.

This is why consistency matters.

This is why mental toughness matters.

Achievement is built in the unseen hours long before anyone claps for you.

ACHIEVEMENT & YOUR FUTURE SELF

Ask yourself:

"What would the next-level version of me do today?"

That version of you:

Shows up on time

Does the hard reps

Thinks long term

Protects their energy

Follows the process

Avoids shortcuts

Builds momentum

Achievement is not something you chase.

It's something you BECOME capable of through disciplined daily action.

THE ACHIEVEMENT CHALLENGE (TAKE ACTION TODAY)

Here is your assignment:

Choose ONE area of your life where you want achievement.

Then write:

✓ The goal

✓ The process

✓ The daily action

✓ The identity you need

✓ The reason it matters

Then begin TODAY — not later.

Achievement belongs to those who start.

Achievement isn't magic.

Achievement isn't luck.

Achievement isn't a gift.

Achievement is earned.

Day by day.

Habit by habit.

Step by step.

Climb by climb.

You have what it takes.

You have the fire (Passion).

You have the potential (Belief).

You have the grit (Mental Toughness).

Now it's time to turn your effort into results.

Let's move forward.

Let's take the next step.

And as always...

Let's keep climbing.

Episode 5

TURNING SMALL WINS INTO BIG WINS

I n this Chapter we're talking about one of the most powerful, overlooked success principles:

Small wins.

Everybody talks about big goals.

Everybody wants massive results.

Everybody wants transformation.

But big wins don't happen without small wins.

And small wins — stacked daily — become the engine behind every major achievement in your life.

Today, we're going to break down:

Why small wins matter

How they rewire your mindset

How small wins turn into momentum

Why they're central to mental toughness

And how to build a daily system that guarantees long-term success

This episode is foundational —

because if you master small wins,

you master growth.

WHY SMALL WINS MATTER MORE THAN BIG ONES

Let's start with a truth that I talk about in Mental Toughness by Coach P Podcast:

Your mind doesn't trust big goals until you prove you can win small.

Everyone wants to:

Lose 30 pounds

Start a business

Become more confident

Change careers

Build discipline

Transform their life

But your brain can't process huge goals without evidence.

Small wins are that evidence.

Each small win sends a signal to your brain:

"I can do this."

"I'm capable."

"I'm moving forward."

"I'm building consistency."

This is why small wins are a central foundation of our Mindset & Mental Performance Course and a major theme running through your upcoming Mental Performance Series Books.

Big wins change your life.

Small wins change you.

THE SCIENCE OF MICRO-MOMENTUM

Small wins do three things neurologically:

1. They release dopamine
Dopamine is the brain's reward chemical.
It makes you feel good about progress.

2. They reinforce positive action loops
Your brain begins to associate action with success.

3. They build identity
Every small win confirms:
"I am the type of person who follows through."
Identity shapes behavior.
Behavior shapes results.
Small wins change identity faster than any motivational speech ever could.

THE "1% BETTER" RULE

Most people overestimate what they can do in a day,

and underestimate what they can do in a year.

If you get 1% better every day,

you don't grow 365% —

you grow over 3,700% because of compounding.

Small wins compound faster than big efforts.

HOW TO START STACKING SMALL WINS

Here's the Coach P formula:

STEP 1 — Identify ONE area you want to improve
Not six areas.
Not all at once.
Just ONE.
Focus builds momentum.

STEP 2 — Choose ONE small win
Examples:
10 push-ups
Drink one bottle of water
Read 2 pages
Journal for 3 minutes
Walk for 5 minutes
Clean one drawer
Write one paragraph
The key is make it so small you can't fail.

STEP 3 — Track your wins
A win that isn't tracked is a win the brain forgets.
Tracking equals proof.
Proof equals belief.
Belief equals momentum.

STEP 4 — Celebrate your progress
Not with rewards —
but with acknowledgment.
"Nice job."
"You followed through."
"You did it again."
Self-recognition builds self-respect.

STEP 5 — Never miss twice
Missing once is human.
Missing twice is a pattern.
Consistency isn't about perfection —
it's about the rule:
We don't miss twice.

HOW SMALL WINS TRANSFORM IDENTITY

Every time you complete a small win, you cast a vote for your next-level identity:

"I'm disciplined."

"I'm consistent."

"I'm improving."

"I'm getting stronger."

"I'm someone who follows through."

This identity shift leads to bigger wins:

Better habits

Bigger goals

Greater confidence

Stronger belief

Higher performance

This is how mental toughness is built — not in giant leaps, but in small steps, consistently repeated.

SMALL WINS IN YOUR DAILY LIFE

Let's get practical.

Where do small wins show up?

In your fitness

Push-ups, water, walking.

In your career

One email, one task, one follow-up.

In your mindset

One page of reading.

One affirmation.

One mental reset.

In your habits

One drawer cleaned.

One step toward organization.

One decision made with intention.

In your relationships

One supportive message.

One act of kindness.

One moment of presence.

Small wins shape every part of life.

THE BIG WIN MYTH

Most people wait for:

The perfect moment

The perfect mindset

The perfect plan

The perfect level of motivation

But perfection is a myth.

Small wins let you START today —

not someday.

Big results come from small reps repeated over time.

Just like we teach in the Goal Setting Course, small daily behaviors are more powerful than big occasional effort.

TODAY'S SMALL WIN CHALLENGE

Here's your challenge for the week:

Choose ONE small win and do it every day for the next 7 days.

Your options:

2 pages of reading

10 push-ups

Drink 20 oz. of water

5 minutes of journaling

Clean one small area

Walk for 6 minutes

The goal is not size.

The goal is consistency.

Small wins become big wins when repeated.

Small wins shape your mindset.

Small wins build your confidence.

Small wins create your momentum.

Small wins transform your identity.

Small wins lead to big wins.

Every big success story you've ever seen —

started with something small.

So today:

Start small.

Stay consistent.

Trust the process.

Build momentum.

Let's take the next step forward.

Let's build wins.

Let's keep climbing.

Episode 6

PURSUING YOUR PURPOSE WITH INTENTIONALITY

n this Chapter we're focusing on one of the most important components of high performance and long-term fulfillment:

Purpose — and more importantly, intentional living.

Passion gives you energy.

Belief gives you internal power.

Small wins build momentum.

But purpose gives your life direction.

Purpose answers the question:

"What am I moving toward?"

And intentionality answers the question:

"How am I moving each day?"

Today we're going to break down:

What purpose really is

How purpose shapes your life

Why most people drift instead of live

How to become intentional

How purpose ties directly to mental toughness

And how to create daily systems that align your actions with your mission

This episode takes your mental performance journey to the next level.

PURPOSE IS YOUR INNER COMPASS

Purpose is not a job.

It's not a task.

It's not a title.

Purpose is direction.

Purpose tells you:

What matters

What deserves your time

What deserves your energy

What deserves your focus

What deserves your discipline

In Mental Toughness by Coach P Podcast, I talk about how purpose creates clarity — and clarity creates power.

When you know WHY you're doing something, you can endure almost anything.

WHY PEOPLE STRUGGLE TO FIND PURPOSE

There are four main reasons:

1. Noise

Life is loud.

Notifications, opinions, distractions, comparison — they drown out your inner voice.

2. Busyness

Most people are too busy reacting to life to take the time to design their life.

3. Fear of choosing wrong

Purpose feels big — and big decisions often trigger hesitation.

4. Disconnection from identity

You cannot know your purpose if you don't know yourself.

And that's why purpose is deeply connected to:

Identity

Belief

Mindset

Confidence

Vision

All of which are pillars of your upcoming Mental Performance Series Books.

YOUR PURPOSE ALREADY EXISTS

People think purpose is something you discover.

It's not.

Purpose is something you unlock.

Inside you is a version of yourself that already knows:

What lights you up

What you care about

What your strengths are

What you're meant to contribute

What direction feels aligned

Most people don't lack purpose —

they lack stillness long enough to hear it.

That's why purpose is such a big focus in both the Passion Course and the Goal Setting Course — they help people quiet the noise and uncover what's already inside.

THE PURPOSE PYRAMID

Purpose has three layers:

1. PASSION — What excites you

Passion is the spark.

Purpose is the direction the spark leads you toward.

2. VALUES — What matters to you

Values tell you what you stand for.

Common purpose-related values include:

Growth

Service

Impact

Leadership

Creativity

Contribution

Faith

Strength

3. MISSION — How you want to use your life

This is where purpose becomes action.

Your mission says:

"This is how I will live.

This is how I will show up.

This is how I will impact others."

Purpose is passion + values + mission.

INTENTIONALITY: THE KEY TO LIVING YOUR PURPOSE

Purpose shows you the direction.

Intentionality drives the vehicle.

Intentionality means:

You choose your habits

You choose your thoughts

You choose your environment

You choose how you spend your time

You choose how you show up

Most people don't live intentionally.

They live reactively.

They react to emotions...

React to distractions...

React to pressure...

React to other people...

React to circumstances...

Intentional people respond with purpose.

***

THE 5 HABITS OF INTENTIONAL PEOPLE

These are the habits I teach in the Mindset & Mental Performance Course and to athletes nationwide.

1. They plan their day before the day begins

Intentional people don't wing it.

2. They protect their energy

They cut out people and habits that drain their mental strength.

3. They say NO more often

Intentional people value alignment over approval.

4. They practice self-awareness

They check in with themselves:

"How am I showing up today?"

5. They follow a system

Intentionality is not vibes — it's structure.

PURPOSE AND HIGH PERFORMANCE

Purpose makes you stronger during adversity.

When things get difficult, purpose becomes your anchor.

When results are slow, purpose keeps you patient.

When obstacles hit, purpose helps you persist.

Purpose is fuel.

Purpose is courage.

Purpose is stability.

HOW TO UNCOVER YOUR PURPOSE

Here's a quick exercise — the same process from your Passion Course:

STEP 1 — Write what gives you energy

What activities light you up?

STEP 2 — Write what the world needs that you care deeply about

Purpose always involves service.

STEP 3 — Write what you are naturally good at

Your gifts point toward your purpose.

STEP 4 — Write the problems you want to help solve

Purpose is found within problems you want to eliminate.

STEP 5 — Write who you want to become

Purpose is tied to identity.

HOW TO LIVE WITH INTENTIONAL PURPOSE DAILY

Here's your daily formula:

1. Start with clarity

"What matters most today?"

2. Choose the TOP 3 actions

Not 20.

Not a giant to-do list.

Three.

3. Remove distractions

Protect the mission.

4. Reflect at night

Ask: "Did I live intentionally today?"

5. Repeat

The repetition transforms your identity.

TODAY'S PURPOSE CHALLENGE

Choose ONE:

Identify your top three values

Define one problem you feel called to solve

Write one line that describes your mission

Identify one distraction you need to eliminate

Plan your next 24 hours intentionally

Purpose becomes clearer through action.

Purpose isn't a mystery.

Purpose isn't accidental.

Purpose isn't for a select few.

Purpose is discovered through reflection,

strengthened through intention,

and lived through consistent action.

You are not here to drift.

You are here to direct your life with purpose, clarity, and intention.

Let's live with purpose today.

Let's stay intentional.

And as always...

Let's keep climbing.

Episode 7

IDENTIFYING WHAT'S HOLDING YOU BACK

I n this Chapter we're talking about one of the most transformative steps in mental performance:

Identifying what's holding you back.

Let me make this clear right from the start:

You cannot fix what you refuse to face.

And you cannot grow past what you won't acknowledge.

Every person — no matter how disciplined, talented, or motivated — as internal and external barriers slowing their progress.

Some you can see. Most you can't.

That's why today's episode is so powerful.

We're going to break down:

What's actually holding you back

How to identify the real source of your limitations

Why people stay stuck

How to remove obstacles

And how this work connects directly to mental toughness, identity, and long-term achievement

Let's get to it.

THE TRUTH ABOUT PROGRESS

Most people don't fail because they aren't capable.

They fail because something is blocking them.

Those blocks may look like:

Distractions

Doubt

Fear

Old habits

Negative people

Lack of clarity

Inconsistent routines

Emotional pain

Low belief

Lack of structure

Here's the part people forget:

You can have big goals... but if you have big anchors tied to your ankles, you're not going anywhere.

In Mental Toughness by Coach P Podcast, I talk about how internal resistance can silently sabotage progress without you realizing it.

Today we're exposing that resistance — so you can finally move past it.

THE 5 MAJOR AREAS THAT HOLD PEOPLE BACK

Let's break down the real reasons people stay stuck.

1. Habits That Don't Match Their Goals

You can't want excellence and practice inconsistency.

You can't want health and practice unhealthy habits.

You can't want discipline and practice avoidance.

Habits either support your future or sabotage it.

2. Self-Doubt & Limiting Beliefs

This one is huge.

Limiting beliefs sound like:

"I'm not good enough."

"What if I fail?"

"I don't deserve success."

"I can't change."

If your belief system doesn't support your goals, you'll always feel resistance.

3. The Wrong Environment

Your environment influences you more than your motivation does.

If you're surrounded by:

Negative people

Complainers

Quitters

Doubters

People who don't want growth

You'll get dragged down.

Environment can either elevate you or suffocate you.

4. Emotional Baggage

Past failures.

Past relationships.

Past criticism.

Past trauma.

Your past may explain you —

but it cannot define you.

However, if you don't face it, it WILL hold you back.

5. Lack of Clarity

When you don't have a plan, you hesitate.

When you hesitate, you lose momentum.

This is why the Goal Setting Course is so powerful — it eliminates fog and gives you structure.

Clarity is freedom.

THE "MIRROR MOMENT" METHOD

Here's a process straight out of the Mental Toughness framework:

Take a moment and ask yourself:

"What part of me is slowing my growth?"

Not:

"Who is to blame?"

"What went wrong?"

"Who hurt me?"

But:

What within me needs to evolve?

This question creates breakthrough-level awareness.

HOW TO UNCOVER WHAT'S REALLY HOLDING YOU BACK

Here's the actual step-by-step process I teach to athletes and clients:

STEP 1 — Identify the Pattern

Look at the last 3 things you quit or avoided.

There's a pattern.

STEP 2 — Identify the Trigger

What emotion or thought shows up before you stop?

Fear?

Overwhelm?

Stress?

Self-doubt?

STEP 3 — Identify the Story

What story do you tell yourself?

"I'll mess this up."

"I'm not ready."

"I'm not disciplined."

"It won't work anyway."

Stories shape actions.

STEP 4 — Identify the Environment

Where do you spend time?

Who do you listen to?

What content are you absorbing?

Environment is shaping your mindset.

STEP 5 — Identify the Missing Skill

Maybe what's holding you back isn't weakness —

maybe it's a skill gap.

Confidence is a skill.

Focus is a skill.

Consistency is a skill.

Planning is a skill.

And the Mental Performance Series Books are designed to teach these skills one at a time.

WHAT YOU TOLERATE BECOMES YOUR LIMIT

This is one of the most important lines of the entire episode:

Your life will rise to the level of what you allow — and fall to the level of what you tolerate.

If you tolerate distraction, you'll produce inconsistency.

If you tolerate self-doubt, you'll produce hesitation.

If you tolerate excuses, you'll produce regrets.

Removing what's holding you back starts with refusing to tolerate the habits and beliefs that limit you.

DOING THE INNER WORK

Removing obstacles isn't glamorous.

It's not Instagram-ready.

It doesn't get applause.

Inner work is quiet.

It's reflective.

It's brave.

Inner work means confronting:

Your fears

Your excuses

Your patterns

Your weaknesses

Your old identity

This is why mental toughness training is so powerful — it gives you the courage to face yourself honestly and grow beyond your limitations.

TODAY'S BREAKTHROUGH EXERCISE

Right now, write down:

"What's the #1 thing holding me back?"

Then write:

"What can I do today to take one step forward?"

One step.

Not the whole solution.

Just the next step.

Breakthroughs begin with honesty —

and accelerate through action.

You are capable of more than your current circumstances.

Your potential is bigger than your obstacles.

Your future is stronger than your past.

But growth requires truth.

And truth requires courage.

Identify what's holding you back...

Release it...

Replace it with strength...

And step into the version of you that you're becoming.

Let's get honest.

Let's get intentional.

And as always…

Let's keep climbing.

Episode 8

HOW TO BUILD UNBREAKABLE CONSISTENCY

n this chapter we're talking about one of the greatest predictors of success in ANY area of life:

Consistency.

Everyone wants results.

Everyone wants improvement.

Everyone wants the breakthrough.

But breakthroughs don't come from doing something big once.

Breakthroughs come from doing something small over and over again — especially when you don't feel like it.

Consistency is the separator.

It's the difference between people who dream...

and people who achieve.

Today we're breaking down:

How consistency is built

Why most people struggle with it

The habits that drive consistency

The mental blocks that destroy consistency

And how to create a daily system that guarantees progress

This Chapter is the heartbeat of achievement.

Let's get started.

CONSISTENCY IS A CHARACTER TRAIT, NOT A FEELING

Most people treat consistency like motivation.

They think:

✓ "I'll be consistent when I feel motivated."

✓ "I'll be consistent when life slows down."

✓ "I'll be consistent when I'm ready."

But consistency doesn't come from emotion.

Consistency comes from character.

It's a daily decision — not a mood.

In Mental Toughness by Coach P Podcast, I talk about how consistency is the bridge between your goals and your results. Without consistency, even the best goals collapse.

Consistency is who you become.

WHY PEOPLE STRUGGLE WITH CONSISTENCY

There are five core reasons:

1. They set goals that are too big

When the goal is massive, it becomes overwhelming.

Overwhelm kills consistency.

2. They rely on motivation

Motivation is unreliable.

Consistency is permanent.

3. They don't have a process

You can't stay consistent without structure.

This is why the Goal Setting Course teaches you how to turn goals into daily behaviors.

4. They don't remove distractions

You can't stay consistent in a chaotic environment.

5. They haven't built a consistent identity

If you see yourself as inconsistent, your actions will match that identity.

Identity is everything.

THE CONSISTENCY PYRAMID

Consistency is built on three layers:

1. Clarity

You must know exactly WHAT needs to be done.

If your plan is vague, your actions will be vague.

2. Structure

Routines.

Systems.

Schedules.

Accountability.

Structure keeps you on track.

3. Standards

This is your internal code.

High standards create high performance.

Standards sound like:

"I show up."

"I finish what I start."

"I don't miss twice."

"I honor my commitments."

This is mental toughness in action.

HOW TO BUILD UNBREAKABLE CONSISTENCY

Here is the Coach P blueprint.

STEP 1 — Start Smaller Than You Think

If you can't do it daily, it's too big.

Every habit should be "so small it's almost embarrassing."

This is how we build consistency in the Mindset & Mental Performance Course — through micro-actions.

STEP 2 — Set a Daily Minimum Standard

No zero days.

Examples:

10 push-ups

2 pages of reading

5 minutes of movement

One journal entry

One small act of kindness

Daily minimums build identity.

STEP 3 — Track Your Progress

Consistency requires visibility.

Write it down.

Check it off.

Mark the calendar.

Tracking builds momentum.

STEP 4 — Eliminate Your Top 3 Distractions

Ask yourself:

"What slows my consistency the most?"

Then remove:

Notifications

Clutter

Negative people

Time-wasting habits

Over-committing

Late nights

Consistency grows where distractions shrink.

STEP 5 — Create an Environment That Supports Success

Your environment must match your goals.

Surround yourself with:

Focus

Growth

Accountability

Energy

Positivity

People who show up

Environment shapes behavior more than motivation ever will.

CONSISTENCY & IDENTITY

Identity is the root of consistency.

You have to say:

"I am a consistent person."

"I follow through."

"I show up."

"I take action even when I don't feel like it."

"I'm built for the climb."

Every consistent action reinforces the identity of a disciplined, focused, mentally tough person.

Identity → Actions → Results → Confidence → More Identity

It's a loop.

And once it clicks, consistency becomes who you are — not something you force.

WHAT CONSISTENCY LOOKS LIKE IN REAL LIFE

Consistency means:

Showing up on the days you don't feel like it

Doing the "boring" reps

Staying focused when nobody's watching

Working in silence

Being patient with progress

Choosing effort over excuses

Staying disciplined when emotions shift

Consistency is not exciting.

Consistency is not glamorous.

Consistency is POWER.

THE CONSISTENCY CHALLENGE

Here's your challenge:

Choose ONE daily habit and do it for the next 14 days.

Examples:

10 push-ups

Read 2 pages

Drink 20 oz. of water

Journal for 3 minutes

Walk for 5 minutes

Clean one small area

Two rules:

1 Don't skip.

2 Don't miss twice.

Consistency is built through repetition — not perfection.

You are capable of extraordinary growth.

You are capable of massive results.

You are capable of becoming the most consistent version of yourself.

But consistency starts today — with one action,

one decision,

one win.

Stack the days.

Stack the habits.

Stack the progress.

Stay focused.

Stay disciplined.

And as always...

Let's keep climbing.

Episode 9

DISCIPLINE OVER MOTIVATION

I n this Chapter we're diving into one of the foundational principles of the Mental Performance lifestyle:

Discipline beats motivation — every single time.

Motivation is a feeling.
Discipline is a decision.

Motivation is temporary.
Discipline is permanent.

Motivation gets you started.
Discipline keeps you going.

Most people struggle not because they're weak — but because they're depending on motivation, which comes and goes like the weather.

If you've ever:

Started strong but fell off

Waited to "feel motivated"

Been inconsistent even when the goal mattered

Or wondered why some people stay locked in while others drift

This episode is for you.

Let's break down why discipline is the weapon of high performers — and how you can build it step by step.

MOTIVATION IS UNRELIABLE

Motivation is emotional.

- You're motivated when:
- You feel inspired
- You hear something powerful
- You get excited
- You start something new
- You feel confident

But motivation disappears when:

- You're tired
- You're stressed
- You're overwhelmed
- You're discouraged
- You're not seeing progress

Motivation cannot be trusted with your goals.

You cannot build a successful life on something that evaporates under pressure.

Motivation is a spark.

Discipline is the fuel.

WHAT DISCIPLINE REALLY IS

Most people think discipline is punishment.

It's not.

Discipline is self-respect.

Discipline says:

✓ "I keep promises to myself."

✓ "I show up regardless of how I feel."

✓ "I don't negotiate with excuses."

✓ "I do the work because the goal matters."

Discipline is the backbone of:

✓ Elite athletes

✓ High-level leaders

✓ Successful entrepreneurs

✓ Great teams

✓ Purpose-driven individuals

And discipline is one of the central themes of Mental Toughness by Coach P Book and the upcoming Mental Performance Series of Books.

THE DISCIPLINE FORMULA

Discipline is built through four components:

1. Clarity

You must know exactly what you want and why it matters.

That's why the Goal Setting Course is so important — it creates a blueprint for your actions.

2. Structure

Discipline thrives with routines:

Morning routine

Workout routine

Work blocks

Reflection time

Daily non-negotiables

Structure creates consistency.

3. Standards

These are your personal rules — the things you no longer negotiate on.

Standards might include:

"I don't miss workouts."

"I read 10 minutes a day."

"I show up early."

"I finish what I start."

"I don't talk myself out of things."

Standards must be higher than your excuses.

4. Self-Respect

This is the heart of discipline.

Say this out loud:

"I deserve the results of discipline."

When you believe that, discipline becomes easier, because you recognize that disciplined actions are acts of self-care.

HOW TO BECOME A DISCIPLINED PERSON

Here's how to build discipline step by step:

STEP 1 — Pick ONE discipline to build

Not five.

Not ten.

Choose one.

STEP 2 — Make the commitment small

Instead of:

"I'll work out an hour a day,"

Start with:

"I'll move for 10 minutes."

Small commitments defeat overwhelm.

STEP 3 — Track it daily

Make it visible.

A simple calendar with checkmarks builds accountability and creates momentum.

STEP 4 — Never miss twice

Missing once is human.

Missing twice becomes a pattern.

This is one of the core rules of the Mindset & Mental Performance Course.

STEP 5 — Attach the discipline to your identity

Say:

"I am a disciplined person."

"I do hard things."

"I show up."

Identity drives behavior.

When you believe you are disciplined,

you act disciplined.

DISCIPLINE & EMOTIONS

Your emotions cannot be trusted with your goals.

Your emotions say:

> "I'm tired."

> "I don't feel like it."

> "I'll start tomorrow."

Discipline says:

> "This matters."

> "We show up."

> "We don't negotiate."

If you wait for motivation, you'll wait forever.

If you train discipline, you'll win.

Discipline isn't a punishment.

Discipline is freedom.

When you build discipline:

✓ You control your mind.

✓ You control your habits.

✓ You control your direction.

✓ You control your results.

✓ You stop wishing.

✓ You start doing.

✓ You stop waiting.

✓ You start winning.

Greatness isn't built on motivation.

Greatness is built on discipline.

Stay disciplined.

Stay focused.

And as always...

Let's keep climbing.

Episode 10

LEARNING TO TRUST YOURSELF AGAIN

n This Chapter we're diving into one of the most powerful and personal topics in all of mental performance:

Learning to trust yourself again.

At some point in life, every person loses trust in themselves.

Maybe you:

Didn't follow through on a goal

Broke a promise

Quit something too early

Stayed in a bad situation too long

Made a mistake that hurt you

Failed publicly

Or repeatedly let yourself down

And when that happens, your internal dialogue starts to shift:

"I can't rely on myself."

"I never finish what I start."

"I don't have the discipline."

"I'm not strong enough."

"I always mess things up."

But here's the truth:

You absolutely can learn to trust yourself again.

You can rebuild confidence.

You can rebuild belief.

You can rebuild your identity.

And today, I'll show you exactly how.

SELF-TRUST IS A SKILL, NOT A PERSONALITY TRAIT

No one is born doubting themselves.

Self-doubt is learned.

Self-trust is also learned.

Which means...

You can train self-trust the same way you train discipline, confidence, and consistency.

Self-trust grows when your actions match your intentions.

Every day you show up — you rebuild trust.

Every time you follow through — you rebuild trust.

Every time you do something hard — you rebuild trust.

This is how we build athletes.

This is how we build leaders.

This is how we build mentally tough people.

HOW SELF-TRUST GETS BROKEN

Self-trust breaks down in small ways, over time.

You lose trust in yourself whenever you:

Make commitments you don't keep

Quit early

Break personal promises

Stay in the wrong environments

Avoid accountability

Let emotions make decisions

Procrastinate on important goals

Repeat habits you said you'd change

Your brain remembers these moments.

But here's the good news:

Your brain also remembers every time you DO follow through.

Which means self-trust is rebuildable — always.

THE "MICRO-PROMISE" SYSTEM

This is one of the most powerful tools we teach in the Mindset & Mental Performance Course because it works fast.

Here's how it works:

You rebuild trust by making micro-promises — tiny commitments that are easy to keep.

Examples:

Drink one bottle of water

Read for five minutes

Do 10 push-ups

Meditate 3 minutes

Clean one small space

Write one encouraging text

Then you repeat them daily.

Micro-promises create micro-wins.

Micro-wins create confidence.

Confidence creates self-trust.

It is simple — but life-changing.

CONSISTENCY CREATES TRUST

Here's the golden rule:

Every time you show up, you tell your mind, "I can count on you."

This is identity shifting.

This is mental rewiring.

This is confidence at its core.

You don't need perfection.

You need repetition.

***

REMOVE THE VOICES THAT BREAK YOUR CONFIDENCE

There are three voices that destroy self-trust:

1. The Voice of Doubt
"Are you sure you can do this?"

2. The Voice of Fear
"What if you fail?"

3. The Voice of Comparison
"You're not as good as they are."
These voices never disappear — but strong people learn to silence them by taking action.

✓ Action kills doubt.

✓ Action kills fear.

✓ Action kills comparison.

You don't fix negative voices by arguing with them.

You fix them by refusing to obey them.

HOW TO REBUILD TRUST AFTER FAILURE

Failure doesn't break your self-trust.

Avoiding action after failure does.

Here's the process:

1. Feel it.

Acknowledge the disappointment.

2. Learn from it.

Failure is information, not identity.

3. Adjust the plan.

Sometimes you didn't fail — the plan did.

4. Take the next step quickly.

Don't retreat.

Don't disappear.

Don't shut down.

Your comeback begins the moment you act again.

THE CONFIDENCE LOOP

Here's how self-trust grows:

Action → Evidence → Confidence → Identity → More Action

This is the exact formula behind our:

Mental Performance Book series

Podcast

Online courses

Coaching philosophy

You don't wait for confidence.

You earn confidence.

You don't wait for belief.

You build belief.

You don't wait to trust yourself.

You act your way into trust.

HOW OUR COURSES BUILD SELF-TRUST

Your online courses are specifically designed to rebuild inner confidence:

PASSION COURSE — Finding Your Dream Job

Helps you reconnect with your deeper purpose.

GOAL SETTING COURSE

Gives you structure and systems that rebuild trust through clarity.

MINDSET & MENTAL PERFORMANCE COURSE

Helps you rewire the internal dialogue that either builds or breaks self-trust.

These courses work together to rebuild self-trust brick by brick — action by action — day by day.

TODAY'S SELF-TRUST CHALLENGE

Here's your assignment:

Choose ONE micro-promise for today.

Just one.

Then keep it.

That's it.

No perfection.

No pressure.

No giant leap.

Just one promise to yourself — honored.

That's how trust begins.

Trusting yourself again isn't an overnight process.

It's a daily process.

You rebuild it with:

Action

Consistency

Honesty

Courage

Discipline

You deserve to trust yourself.

Your future self is counting on you.

Your goals require a version of you who believes in your own strength.

So show up today — not for perfection,

but for proof.

Let's rebuild belief.

Let's strengthen confidence.

And as always...

Let's keep climbing.

Episode 11

CONTROLLING THE CONTROLLABLES

n this chapter we're diving deep into one of the most important skills in all of mental performance, leadership, athletics, business, and life:

Controlling the controllables.

This mindset separates the emotionally reactive from the mentally strong.

It separates people who get overwhelmed from people who get focused.

And it separates those who stay stuck... from those who keep climbing.

Today you'll learn:

Why controlling the controllables builds instant confidence

How to stop wasting energy on things you can't change

How elite performers simplify their minds

How to master the "circle of control"

And how this single shift can transform your results

Let's get into it.

THE WORLD IS FULL OF UNCONTROLLABLES

Life is constantly throwing things at you that you cannot control:

Other people

Their decisions

Their opinions

Their effort

Their attitude

The past

Unexpected events

Weather

Delays

Setbacks

Timing

Outcomes

If you focus on these things,

you will always be frustrated.

If you try to control these things,

you will always feel powerless.

Mental toughness begins the moment you accept this truth:

You don't control everything —

but you DO control the things that matter most.

THE CIRCLE OF CONTROL

Every situation contains three circles:

1. The Circle of Control

These are the things ONLY you control:

Your attitude

Your effort

Your energy

Your reactions

Your habits

Your standards

Your preparation

Your decisions

Your focus

Your self-talk

Your discipline

This is where winners live.

2. The Circle of Influence

Things you can guide or impact, but not control:

Your team

Your home environment

Your workplace culture

Your friendships

Your schedule

Your routines

You influence these by how YOU show up.

3. The Circle of No Control

Things completely outside your hands:

Past mistakes

Weather

Economy

Timing

People's opinions

Other people's behaviors

Unexpected challenges

Focusing here drains your energy, destroys clarity, and weakens confidence.

The mentally tough eliminate the third circle and live in the first two.

WHY PEOPLE STRUGGLE WITH CONTROL

People lose control because they:

1. Try to manage everything

This leads to overwhelm.

2. Care too much about approval

You can't control how people see you.

3. Fear uncertainty

When the future feels unclear, people try to grip everything.

4. Avoid responsibility

It's easier to blame than to own your effort.

5. Mistake chaos for complexity

When things feel chaotic, people think the solution is complicated.

But the truth is powerful:

Control is simple —

not easy,

but simple.

CONTROLLING THE CONTROLLABLES BUILDS CONFIDENCE

Here's why this matters:

When you control what YOU can control, you create:

Confidence

Clarity

Momentum

Emotional stability

Focus

Resilience

A sense of power

Inner peace

People don't lose confidence because they're weak.

They lose confidence because their mind is focused on things they cannot influence.

This is why controlling the controllables is a major theme in:

Mental Toughness by Coach Podcast

The Mindset & Mental Performance Course

Multiple books in our Mental Performance Series

Confidence grows when your energy goes to the right places.

HOW TO MASTER "CONTROL" IN DAILY LIFE

Here's the Coach P system:

STEP 1 — Ask: "What can I control right now?"

This question instantly removes emotional chaos.

It diverts you from fear → focus.

STEP 2 — Take ownership

Take responsibility for your half of the situation.

Ownership = power.

STEP 3 — Redirect your energy

Move energy AWAY from:

Worry

What-if thinking

Other people's behavior

Imagined outcomes

The past

And move energy TOWARD:

Action

Preparation

Effort

Attitude

Solutions

STEP 4 — Establish controllable daily habits

Examples:

Morning routine

Time-blocked work

Daily gratitude

10 minutes of reading

15 minutes of movement

Standard bedtime

Hydration goals

Tracking progress

These habits create internal control.

STEP 5 — Recenter when emotions rise

When stress hits, say:

"Control what I can control.

Release what I can't."

Repeat until your mind reset.

HOW THIS CHANGES YOUR PERFORMANCE

In athletics, business, and life, controlling the controllables:

Sharpens focus

Increases output

Reduces stress

Eliminates excuses

Strengthens leadership

Enhances teamwork

Improves relationships

Builds mental toughness

The strongest people are not the ones who control everything —

they're the ones who control themselves.

THE MENTAL PERFORMANCE SERIES CONNECTION

Several of our upcoming books will be built around this theme:

Our entire Mental Performance series of books teaches people how to take back control of their:

Mind

Behavior

Emotions

Habits

Environment

Direction

This is foundational work.

TODAY'S CONTROL RESET

Take something that's bothering you right now.

Ask:

1. What part of this can I control?

2. What part can I influence?

3. What part do I need to let go of?

4. What one action can I take today?

This simple reset changes everything.

When life feels chaotic,

control what you can.

When emotions rise,

control what you can.

When pressure hits,

control what you can.

Your power is not in controlling the world — it's in controlling yourself.

Attitude.

Effort.

Energy.

Focus.

Response.

Standards.

Actions.

This is mental toughness.

This is leadership.

This is growth.

Stay focused.

Stay grounded.

And as always...

Let's keep climbing.

Episode 12

BUILDING RESILIENCE: BOUNCING BACK STRONGER

n this Chapter we are tackling a topic that every champion, every high-performer, and every person striving for greatness must master:

Resilience — the ability to bounce back stronger.

Life is not about avoiding adversity.

It's about learning to rise through it.

Setbacks don't define you.

Storms don't break you.

Pressure doesn't weaken you.

Your response determines your strength.

Your resilience determines your future.

Today we're going to break down:

What resilience actually is

Why some people rise while others fall

The difference between failing and quitting

How to recover from setbacks

How to build "bounce-back strength"

And how resilience fits into the Mental Performance lifestyle

Let's get into it.

WHAT RESILIENCE REALLY IS

Resilience is not:

Being perfect

Being emotionless

Being unbreakable

Ignoring pain

Hiding failure

Resilience is the ability to:

Feel pain but not give up

Take hits and keep moving

Fall but rise again

Adapt under pressure

Refocus after disappointment

Grow through struggle

Resilience is strength built through adversity.

In Mental Toughness by Coach P Podcast, I talk about how adversity does not weaken you — it introduces you to the strongest version of yourself.

WHY RESILIENCE MATTERS

Every major success in life will demand resilience:

Achieving a goal

Pursuing a dream

Leading others

Starting a business

Changing habits

Improving your health

Building confidence

Developing discipline

Resilience is the foundation that allows you to stay in the game long enough to win.

Most people don't fail because they aren't capable —

they fail because they don't bounce back.

THE 4 TYPES OF SETBACKS

Understanding the setback helps you rise from it.

1. Emotional Setbacks

Moments of self-doubt, insecurity, fear, overwhelm, or stress.

2. Circumstantial Setbacks

Unexpected events you didn't choose —

injury, loss, finances, environment.

3. Habit Setbacks

Loss of consistency, slipping into old patterns, procrastination.

4. Performance Setbacks

Mistakes, failures, or outcomes that don't go your way.

Resilience is built by confronting these setbacks with intention instead of avoidance.

HOW RESILIENT PEOPLE THINK

Resilient people think VERY differently from those who break under pressure.

Resilient people say:

✓ "This is tough, but it's temporary."

✓ "I will grow from this."

✓ "I can figure this out."

✓ "I've overcome before, I'll overcome again."

Resilient people don't ask:

"Why is this happening TO me?"

They ask:

"What is this teaching me?

How can I grow from this?"

That shift is EVERYTHING.

THE RESILIENCE LOOP

Here's the exact cycle resilient people follow:

Struggle → Reflection → Adjustment → Action → Growth → Strength

This loop is repeated every time adversity hits.

Without reflection, you repeat mistakes.

Without adjustment, you stay stuck.

Without action, you lose belief.

The loop must stay active.

And that is why your Mindset & Mental Performance Course works — it trains your brain to stay engaged in the resilience cycle.

THE 5 SKILLS THAT BUILD RESILIENCE

Here is the Coach P formula:

1. Self-Awareness

Recognize what you're feeling and why.

2. Emotional Control

Don't let emotions dictate your actions.

Control the controllables.

3. Adaptability

Change the plan when needed — but NEVER the mission.

4. Persistence

Refuse to quit.

Refuse to retreat.

Refuse to fold under pressure.

Persistence often beats talent.

5. Confidence

Confidence comes from proving to yourself that you can bounce back.

You can't build confidence without resilience.

HOW TO BOUNCE BACK FROM FAILURE

Here's the process:

STEP 1 — Pause and breathe.

Don't react in emotion.

STEP 2 — Reflect honestly.

What really happened?

Where did things break down?

STEP 3 — Extract the lesson.

Ask:

"What can I learn from this?"

STEP 4 — Adjust the strategy.

Refine the plan, not the dream.

STEP 5 — Take the next step quickly.

Comebacks begin with action.

The longer you wait, the heavier the moment becomes.

Bounce-back strength comes from decision, not delay.

RESILIENCE AND IDENTITY

Resilience shifts your identity in a powerful way.

Every time you rise after struggle, your identity upgrades:

"I am strong."

"I am capable."

"I can handle adversity."

"I'm not someone who quits."

"I bounce back."

Identity fuels performance.

Look for our upcoming Mental Performance Series Books on identity, discipline, and mindset — will help readers build this resilient identity step-by-step.

THE ADVERSITY ADVANTAGE

Strong people don't just survive adversity — they USE it.

Resilience turns adversity into:

Fuel

Wisdom

Strength

Character

Focus

Purpose

Adversity becomes the advantage.

Champions aren't built in comfort — they're built in the climb.

RESILIENCE CHALLENGE

Here's your assignment:

Think of ONE setback from the last 30 days.

Then write these four things:

1. What happened?

2. What did it teach you?

3. What can you adjust?

4. What is the very next step?

When you take that next step — you win.

Resilience is not about avoiding struggle.

Resilience is about rising stronger because of struggle.

You have survived 100% of your hardest days.

You're tougher than you think.

You're stronger than you realize.

You're built for the climb and built for the comeback.

Whatever you're facing — you can get through it.

You can grow from it.

You can rise above it.

Stay resilient.

Stay committed.

And as always...

Let's keep climbing.

ABOUT THE AUTHOR

COACH P. JIM PUSATERI** brings over 65 years of hard-knocks life experience to his work as a mentor and performance coach. Having faced and overcome real-world challenges, he now dedicates his life to helping others develop the mental strength needed to rise above adversity and move forward with confidence.

He is the author of *PASSION BELIEF ACHIEVEMENT: YOUR MINDSET IS YOUR GREATEST WEAPON*, a powerful guide to mastering your mindset and unlocking your full potential. He previously published *Mental Toughness: The Ability to MOVE FORWARD Under Pressure*, a foundational work focused on resilience, discipline, and performing under pressure.

Through his coaching, teaching, and writing, Coach P. Jim Pusateri equips individuals with practical tools to build passion, strengthen belief, and achieve lasting success — proving that with the right mindset, no obstacle is insurmountable.